Being Pushed To Your Destiny

WIYANA BAILEY

Being Pushed To Your Destiny

Have you been pushed?

ReadersMagnet, LLC

Being Pushed To Your Destiny
Copyright © 2022 by Wiyana Bailey

Published in the United States of America
ISBN   Paperback: 978-1-959165-70-5
ISBN   eBook: 978-1-959165-71-2

All rights reserved. No part of this publication may be reproduced, stored in a retrieval system or transmitted in any way by any means, electronic, mechanical, photocopy, recording or otherwise without the prior permission of the author except as provided by USA copyright law.

The opinions expressed by the author are not necessarily those of ReadersMagnet, LLC.

ReadersMagnet, LLC
10620 Treena Street, Suite 230 | San Diego, California, 92131 USA
1.619. 354. 2643 | www.readersmagnet.com

Book design copyright © 2022 by ReadersMagnet, LLC. All rights reserved.

Cover design by Ericka Obando
Interior design by Dorothy Lee

ACKNOWLEDGMENTS

To my late parents, Saundra Spearmon and Willie Harris, I'm saddened that you couldn't be here to experience my life as it is today. I truly appreciate the life that was given, and I will always love you both dearly. To my grandmother, Ruth Griffin-Holliday, I want to thank you for the strength that you did show. Although you're no longer here, I know your eyes are resting heavily upon us. To my three lovely children—Tromaneshia, Everett, and Janay—thank you all for the strength and motivation you bring out of your mother. To my closest sibling, Agar Jackson, Denise vet, and Stephen Harris, your spiritual life still has always shined bright upon my life. You have always been a great influence on me.

For my family, finally, my husband, who always supports and have my back. I love you, Floyd Bailey. Special thanks to Nellie Chaney. Words can't explain how much I appreciate and love you for pushing me to pursue bigger things and the role you played in my life. For my church family of Brown Memorial Church of God in Christ, thank you for your continued guidance.

TABLE OF CONTENTS

1 The Push 9
2 Motherhood 15
3 Real Life 19
4 Changes 23
5 Bigger and Better 27
6 Being Driven 29

Introduction

My name is Wiyana Bailey, Being Push to your Destiny came in the form of in school one night (College) which eventually led to this book. It was good for me that I was afflicted that I might learn thy statutes Psalm 119:67-69,71. First and foremost, God! His presence joined me on the spiritual journey that became being push. I thank you lord for your inspiration and your love, writing this book has cost myself and family both time and a journey into adventure and emotion. But it has been a worthwhile journey! Realizing how everyone vitally need this information. I am sure that many outwardly successful but inwardly troubled people will be greatly help by reading this book. Like the silhouette on the cover, most people spend their entire lives chasing something they already have. However, the book of Being Push to your Destiny written from an entirely different perspective with my strengths and weaknesses before me, I needed to be push so that I could sort it all out and move forward. Understanding and Being Mindful of what I want us of life help me to consider priorities and arrange my life with eternal objective in mind. Discover myself live passionately and boldly, now I ask Have You Being Push?

1

WB
The Push

Some may look at being pushed as a physical push, what you can see. The push I'm speaking about is a mental push that starts with an act of thinking of the mind as a powerful force. The mind is set of cognitive faculties that enable consciousness, perception, thinking, judgment, and memory—a characteristic of humans; the part of faculty of a person by which one feels, perceives, desires, and imagines studying the relation between the brain and the mind. The mind is a terrible thing to waste and a good thing to invest in.

Nevertheless, you shall love the Lord your God with all your heart, with all your soul and with all your mind. This is the greatest and first commandment. The pushes we receive in life will build our character for who we are and whom we become. I could remember as early as six years of age, my mother would come into my room every morning, and she'll say, "Okay, it's time to get up to get ready for school!" My body would just lie there only to hear her come in once again with a different tone of voice. Just her tone alone pushed my little body up and helped me to get ready to face the world every morning. She made sure I was up and at the bus stop in a timely manner so I would not miss the bus to school. When I didn't know the importance of going to bed early, get plenty of rest to prevent me from being tired in class and the importance of getting up early.

My mother was a single parent with two children and with her own issues that she was facing despite of her problems she may have had. I thank God for her being able to see the importance of our needs. My sister and I prayed to the Lord every night. We were never taught how to pray, but we had faith and believed in our prayer that God would answer. We prayed so we will have a peaceful night. There were times where we prayed until our hands would sweat. Proverbs 3:24 (asv) said, "When thou liest down, thou shalt not be afraid: Yea, thou shalt lie down, and they sleep be sweet." The moment we didn't pray, that's when the abuse would slip in. Drinking was the number-one factor. We never knew what the next day would bring.

I can recall times when my mother would allow me to stay home from school for an illness at the beginning of the school year, and she would wait until the end of the school year to chastise me for what she allowed to happen. She would ask for my sister to come for her to be chastised for bringing two papers home. The papers were for her assignment to be corrected. Her teacher gave her another chance to do it again, but our mother looked at it as if she stole the paper. We were two nervous children. "For God gave us not a spirit of fearfulness; but of power and love and discipline" (2 Tim. 1:7, asv).

However, mother's, it's okay to ask for help. There are places that can provide assistance to you such as parenting classes online, friends, church, or a family member. These are a few resources you can utilize.

Being Pushed To Your Destiny

Life has a way of changing our children. Our youth are our future. We are all responsible for one another to ensure our children are gaining the proper knowledge. Rather you're a teacher, a parent, an aunt, cousin, or uncle, this is something we can all play a part in helping. "Train up a child in the way he should go, and even when he is old he will not depart from it" (Prov. 22:6, asv). Once children hit their adolescent age, they can be so brutal. They are unaware of the effect negative words can have on the next individual. A child's negativity can unknowingly cause someone to see themselves in a different light, which, in fact, can result in things, such as low self-esteem and lack of confidence, which can follow one into adulthood.

Therefore, parents must be mindful of what is being deposited into their children. No, we can't be there 24-7, but it's important to have a sit-down talk with them. Doing little activities helps to build rapport with your child. Activities such as having a date with your child(ren), asking about their day, even writing notes and letters for them to respond back to are good ideas. Also, adapting habits such as having dinner together as a family will help your children become more open and free to express themselves. It also helps your child realize it's a difference between how you talk and how you write.

Parents should also consider getting the kids involved into extracurricular activities. Everything doesn't involve costs and fees. Something as simple as getting involved in the church is free, which may be the best resort. We pay for cheerleading, soccer, and football when the church offers free activities such as becoming a member of the choir, becoming an usher, and attending Sunday school, which is commensurate with private lessons. "I can do all things in him that strengthen me" (Phil. 4:13, asv).

Some things in life you will learn you have no control over. You will find out that there will be times where mother may not be there to push you. So, if you're fortunate enough to get that extra support, accept it. Unfortunately, there are those who never had a parent to lend a helping hand, or one may have fell into hard times. There are cases where parents are undergoing some type of addiction problems or suffering from tragedies.

Lean on trust in and be confident in the Lord with all your heart and mind and do not rely on your own insight or understanding. In all your ways know recognize and acknowledge him he will direct and make straight and plain your paths. (Prov. 3:5–6, amp) Now time progresses. You're older, and you're encountering different obstacles. You may feel that you've aged, and you think there isn't a need to be pushed anymore by anyone. You try to embrace what needs to be done and prioritize when necessary. However, when you reach an age of legitimacy, you may feel a bit more liberated. You no longer have anyone to answer to. You can hang out and stay out as late as you want. Entering adulthood is like freedom knocking on your door, and it's up to you to make the right decision. As we all know, this is easier said than done. This is how the enemy works. He will show you all things that look good, feel good, sound good but don't let you see the result.

We know that the law is spiritual; but I am a creature of the flesh [carnal, unspiritual], having been sold into slavery under [the control of] sin. For I do not understand my own actions [I am baffled, bewildered]. I do not practice or accomplish what I wish, but I do the very thing that I loathe [which my moral instinct condemns]. Now if I do [habitually] what is contrary to my desire, [that means that] I acknowledge and agree that the law is good (morally excellent) and that I take sides with it. However, it is no longer I who do the deed, but the sin [principle] which is at home in me and has possession of me. (Rom. 7:14–17, amp) Just when you thought you didn't need guidance, you find out time is extremely valuable, and you must maintain a level of responsibility. Again, prioritize. Dedicating time to study is very vital to your learning. Rather you're studying for an exam or studying your Bible. Reading is fundamental, so why not feed your knowledge? As they say, "A mind is a terrible thing to waste." In retrospect, you'll always have time to have fun.

There will be time to go on dates and hang out with friends. There's always time for that. Just be cognizant of your time management on a larger scale. The more time you devote into your well-being will set you up for a better future. Invest in your education, work toward your career goals, and grow spiritually. Focusing more on these things will give you a better outlook on life. However, it is understood that everyone should enjoy their lives.

Time management doesn't mean exempt activities out; it means to find a balance that'll help you reach your goal.

BEING PUSHED TO YOUR DESTINY

Do not be conformed to this world (this age), [fashioned after and adapted to its external, superficial customs], but be transformed(change) by the [entire] renewal of your mind [by its new ideals and its new attitude], so that you may prove {for yourselves} what is the good and acceptable and perfect will of God, even the thing which is good and acceptable and perfect {in his sight for you}. (Rom. 12:2, amp) We must condition our mind on whom we allow ourselves to be brainwashed. There will be someone to have an influence on you who will start from changing how you see things. It's up to you what type of washing you will receive— normal, gentle, or permanent press. What's your level of capacity—small, medium, super, or your temperature—cold, warm, or hot.

"So, because you are lukewarm and neither cold nor not I will spew you out my mouth" (Rev. 3:16, amp).

The renewal of your mind cleanses your thought pattern for those occasions where there's a need to change your mind-set. You may not realize it now, but a lot of times, you need a mental push. You need someone to bring out what's in you all along. Thinking back, I lost four years of opportunities not taking advantage of what I had in front of me. I was a teenager who dropped out of school during the first nine weeks of my freshman year of high school. I was involved in a relationship, which in fact was not healthy for me nor my education. I was being pushed, and I was being influenced. Having a boyfriend now was not in my best interest. In this instance, it helped me to understand that the push and/or influence you receive may not be all good but an experience of learning and knowing what is good for you.

The key is to learn from it. Always remember, if you feel that a push you receive will be dealt unto you, please remove yourself out of that situation quickly. Although I missed out on a lot, I also learned a lot. Sometimes, we take life for granted, and we allow opportunities to pass us by. We know that what God has for us will be for us. It's important to give yourself a chance to experience and expand. In some cases, experience may take you further than education, so imagine where you can be in life if you combine the two.

Tell yourself you deserve better. You are better, and you will see well. Don't allow your situation to determine your destiny or who you will become. Every situation is a set up for where you are going. You may not see it now, but you will later.

2

WB
Motherhood

As time progressed, I was then a parent experiencing motherhood. I had no idea how to really be a mother. I just learned different habits and figured out what worked best for us. Morals and principles were instilled in me at a young age by my own mother who was murdered at the age of twenty-eight. At that time, I was only at the tender age of ten. Just with that little time being in my life, she made sure that we had a solid foundation for myself and sister. We learned respect. When speaking to our elders, we were to respond with, "No, ma'am," or "Yes, ma'am." Not even just our elders but also the general people around. In addition to that, we had structure. There was a set bedtime, a set time to wake up in the morning for school, and we understood that our rooms had to and would be cleaned before we left. Even after school hours, we had the option to go outside and play, but we had better make sure that we were in the house before the streetlights came on. We didn't have any watches or cell phones; we were just very aware. These things were learned habits and things that I deposited into my child.

As a parent, we sometimes want to compromise with our children. We want to honor their needs and wants. However, there will be times for compromise, and there is always time for parenting. Some parents may feel that the child isn't deserving of an explanation as to why Mom or Dad said no. There are others who would rather explain to the child why this isn't the best thing for them. It's important to always keep their best interest at heart. Our children are our future. Make sure they understand that it's not okay to stay or go over a friend's house without a parent's approval and not to walk the streets alone at night. Even if your child feels comfortable enough to ask someone for money, make sure you're aware that it's not a stranger. It's a crazy world we live in, and we want our children to be as safe and protected as possible. Everyone has their own unique style of parenting. These are just things that I've experienced to help me as a parent.

The giving of my love gives my children power and strength during their weaknesses. I push them to see what they may not see in themselves. I set fire in them as opposed to under them. The love you feel for your kids is immersible, they are the beat of your heart, the blood in your veins and the energy of your soul. There is nothing greater than the love you have for your kid is the reason I keep going even when things get tough and they give you more strength every day.

You'll then realize that they'll start to make their own decisions that they feel will be best. Reflecting, there was a time where I was out drinking, doing drugs, and clubbing. I went out with family members to have good time, and a good time turned into a bad time. I ended up back home with someone I didn't know. I had no idea who the guy was who took me back home. I was so consumed with alcohol I vomited in his car. I can hear him saying, "You messing up my car!" I pleaded with him to take me home, and by the grace of God, he did just that—took me home.

Just that quickly, my life could've taken a turn for the worse. In fact, that person could've kidnapped and or murdered me. Temporary decisions can change our life forever. Was this the best decision that I made? No. Was it my decision? Yes. The moral of the story is what our youth may see as just having fun could lead to different pathways.

Now all choices aren't bad. It may seem easier to do what's wrong instead of what's right but doing the right thing will never fail you. You may not see it now, but you will later. After dropping out of school and taking some time off, I decided to get back to it and proceed where I left off. I went ahead and attended night school and made it to receive my high school diploma. Not only was I attending night school, I was also working at Tampa General Hospital. I worked there for sixteen years. So many of my coworkers saw well in me. They saw something in me that I didn't see in myself, but they had a funny way of showing it. I was told that I would be fired if I didn't go back to finish school, so I knew for sure that I needed to go back before I got fired and risk losing the only job I had. At that time, I worked in a laundry facility. However, I was naive to the fact that there weren't any education requirements, so I went ahead and enrolled into night school. I didn't want to do it, but I did.

Every day, as soon as I would clock in for work, someone will come and ask me, "Little girl, did you go to school last night?"

So, to keep from telling a lie, I made sure I was in attendance to every class. There was so and still is so much respect I have for this woman. Every time I saw her and when I would consider her eyes, I was happy to say, "Yes, I attended school last night." She supported me like a mother, and she helped me to stay on track. I knew not to disrespect her, and I did not want to disappoint her.

Sometimes you must learn how to decipher who's there to help push you in the right direction and find out how to accept that push. When you have, someone pushing you to better yourself, take advantage of it. Trust me, you will always be so grateful for the concern of those who really have your best interest at heart. At one point, I was saying "just leave me alone" to myself because it can be very annoying having someone constantly on you about doing what you really don't want to do. The thing to understand is you may not see it now, but you will later. Humble yourself. Realize who's going to steer you to the right path. If you are unsure, pray for guidance.

3

WB
Real Life

Ever dreamed about being wealthy—not having to work but being able to travel the world and experience new things and buy nice cars and beautiful homes? Ever had a chance to really dream? Ever had a chance to sit back and think, what do I really want out of this life? Think about where you are going in life, what career path are you going to choose, and how can you make this happen. Start small and build your way up. If not, start by setting small goals for yourself, something short term that you know you can achieve and surpass. Something as simple as setting a time to go to bed at the same time every night to wake up on time the next morning and be sure to have your clothing prepared the night before are simple goals to start off with. Then start thinking bigger and long term. If you're innovative, consider becoming an entrepreneur. Everyone has their level of skill set and talents, and we all have gifts that are instilled in us. It's our job to utilize the gift given to us. Pray and ask for guidance and a vision; he knows what works best. Imagine having created the first line of hair products for African American women like our late great Madam C. J. Walker. Learning about history can influence you greatly. To think that someone living in such hard times made it to be an entrepreneur, philanthropist, and all-around successful person is completely inspiring. We should all take the time to learn about our history. Lack of knowledge could lead to lack of direction. We all have destiny hidden inside of us that shine so bright to the right object.

Let your light so shine before men, that they may see your good works, and glorify your father which is in heaven (Matthew 5:16 kjv).

Furthermore, through learning more about yourself, figuring out what your likes and hobbies are, you may find that you have unidentified interests. You may find that you do good job with your hair or even doing your kids' hair, so there's a possibility you can go into the field of cosmetology. Why not take a shot at it? Enrolling into beauty school is quick and, for some, easy. This is how I got my start. From an early start of playing with dolls, I knew I had an interest. I decided to attend school and earn my cosmetology license. However, it wasn't so easy for me. There were times where I just didn't feel like getting up to go, any and every obstacle tried to block my path. There were times where I didn't have any gas to get to school. I didn't even have a babysitter on certain occasions. These hiccups caused me to not receive all the hours that was needed to pass at the end. This meant more school.

Dedication is key. If you want it, you should go out and get it. Don't let time pass you by. Before you know it, it's three years later, and you are finally returning to school, and guess what? Now it's time to take the big exam. In my case of cosmetology, it was the state board exam. Considering that the first half of my education was years prior, I was a bit rusty on my knowledge of some of the book work. Even still I felt good about the test. I knew for sure that I would go in, sit for the hour-long test, and ace it. I took studying for granted. I thought I had it all worked out. After finishing and getting results, I realized I didn't pass. The first failure was disappointing, but I knew that there was always opportunity to retake the exam for a better score, so I did.

Again, I went in with a positive mind to pass, and you wouldn't believe the results. I failed again. Now the saying is that the third time is usually the charm. I then became serious. I had to tell myself there was no way I did all this work to fail and come all this way to turn back. I ended up having to commit more hours to school, and most importantly, I prayed. I asked the Lord to please help me pass that test. It was like I heard the Lord say, I can't bring anything back to your memory that you haven't even committed to study. I went home and got right in the books like never.

As time passed, it was four years later since starting on a course that was only to last a year and a half, and I finally finished. This goes to show of how we can't give up on our dreams. I now am a licensed cosmetologist and owner of a beauty salon. Every new day is another chance. "I have strengthened for all things in Christ who empowers me" (Phil. 4:13, asv).

I am ready for anything and equal to anything through him who infuses inner strength into me. I am self-sufficient in Christ's sufficiency.

4

WB
Changes

To change your life is unfolding from the pushes. Before starting my own business, I was pondering renting a booth at another salon. For whatever reason, I put working in a salon on the back burner. I was still in the swing of going out and partying, so my head wasn't completely screwed on tight just yet. Every time I would go out, I found myself always getting into a confrontation with someone about something. It just wasn't the same anymore. The vibe was just different. It was a sign that was no longer the scenery for me, and I didn't want what happened to my mother to happen to me. I can recall a very Sunday morning where my youngest daughter looked up and asked, "Can we go to church this morning?" I had a hangover, and I was sluggish, but how could I have denied her of going to church? So, I said, "Yes, we can go," not knowing that same day, I was going to accept Christ. It was October 14, 1999. Once I got back to the house, everything I thought was not godly had to go; even down to relationship. My life changed so dearly I prepared myself to have my own home and to even get off section 8.

Instantly, I had a mind to do what was in the best interest of myself and my children. I had a plan to pay any debt that I owed.

Any unpaid funds that were sent to the credit bureau, I planned to pay them off. I wanted to get to a decent credit score where I could be eligible to buy a house. That way, my kids would have a place to call home. I put my mind to it, and that's exactly what I did.

God always has someone there to help you along the way. A friend of mine gave me the contact information to a realtor, and I stayed in contact with her for about a year. We searched around, looking for a nice area and place we could call home. I wasn't too pleased initially. I just couldn't seem to find exactly what I was looking for. I so happened to reach out to my realtor, and I asked her if there were any more options available than the ones presented, and thank goodness, there were. Two new homes had just been posted, and I couldn't wait to go out and see them. We viewed the first home, and it was perfect. It had just what I wanted—three bedrooms, one-and-a half bath, and a flora room with a living room, patio, and a big yard. I had never bought a home before, so I went to consult with my aunt before making any decisions. By the time, we made up our minds to go with the house, it was unfortunately already sold. I was heartbroken.

The good news was, there was still a shot at finding the right house. I had one more to view. I went home and prayed. Once I opened the Bible, it automatically opened to Matthew 7:7. That alone gave me peace. We pulled to the house number two.

I thought, I guess this one is okay. Considering the bedrooms through the windows, I thought they were small.

Then the realtor pulled up and asked, "Would you like to look inside?" I wasn't feeling as excited as I was about the first house, but once we entered inside, it was wonderful! Like wow. She said this house was renovated. There was a new roof, four bedrooms, one-and-a-half bath, and central AC unit.

My first reaction was, "Yes, let's sign now." I didn't want this one to pass me by. Soon, as I got in the car, I still wanted to ask my aunt and see how she felt about this house, and as I listened to the radio, there was a preacher speaking on "why are you questioning God and what God is already giving you," I felt that was a confirmation for me. I knew this was for me.

Now we were moving forward to do the closing cost. I only had my check, which was already gone before I received it, so I said, "I'll go get a loan from the credit union." I went over to the credit union, completed the loan application, and I was denied. I couldn't get a loan from anyone, and no one would lend me the money. I asked God how I could be approved for a $61,000 home, and I couldn't even find $5,000 to get it. By this time, I was very nervous about getting back with the realtor. Some people may ask why you go looking for a house without any money. The answer is I had faith. I believed this was going to work for me. "So also, faith, if it does not have works [deeds and actions of obedience to back it up], by itself is destitute of power [inoperative, dead]" (James 2:17, amp).

Well, there I was, returning the call to the realtor with the expectation of bad news from her, asking about the closing cost. I wasn't going to allow not having the funds to stop me, so I proceeded with the call.

She answered, saying, "Ms. Harris, I have your papers ready for your closing." I stopped her right then, and I told her, "I'm sorry, but I don't have any money for my closing."

What came out of her mouth next, I couldn't believe. She responded, "No, Mrs. Harris, you only need two hundred dollars for the closing of your new home for now, and the remaining will divided thereafter." Tears started to fall down my face. I couldn't believe what I was hearing, and I couldn't help but to be so thankful. "Keep on asking and it will be given you; keep on seeking and you will find; keep on knocking [reverently] and [the door] will be opened to you" (Matt. 7:7, amp).

The big announcement was revealed to my children that we are moving into our new home, thanks to low-income housing and section 8, which was my stepping stone. I look at being in the project community as a teaching tool of responsibility of paying bills to keep a roof over your family. I saw this government assistance program as preparation to get yourself in your own home. They gave the option to move in to a nicer house, and it helped me to set my goals higher. I saw an opportunity, and I was ready to take advantage of it to make it work for me and my family. Before we knew it, we were all settled in our first new home. I changed the school the kids were attending, and they got an opportunity to meet new friends and new neighbors in our new neighborhood. Oh, what a good feeling to start with a new beginning in one phase of life.

YOU'RE ALWAYS ONE DECISION AWAY FROM A TOTALLY DIFFERENT LIFE.

5

WB
Bigger and Better

I'm ready to work in a shop, and my ambition was in full force. You have to be strong hard-working later you carry many responsibilities on your shoulder but you do it all and find ways to get everything done.

I searched around to find a good place to work. Someone told me about a shop around the way and told me to go and check it out. So, I decided to go over and see how things were. I went there, and right away, I felt welcomed. I accepted the offer to become an employee, and I worked there for six years. During the time, I was there, so many people were saying that eventually, I would have my own beauty shop. One of the ladies would always tease me about driving in luxury cars, and we all would just laugh. I didn't really think much of it. There was also another lady who asked if I would like to open a shop with her. I considered the offer because she and I worked so well. I thought more about it, and I didn't go through because I didn't want this to just be a spare-of-the-moment type of ordeal. However, this caused something in me to start stirring to open my own spot. In the mix of looking for a salon, my sister and I decided to open a beauty supply store. The store was up and running for a year. This was my first business but not my goal. Sometimes, in life, we go in different directions, and as always, we should continue to look forward.

By now, I was pretty content with how things were going. I was enjoying working at the shop and working at Tampa General Hospital, and that's where my husband found me. "He who finds a [true] wife finds a good thing and obtains favor from the Lord" (Prov. 18:22, amp). After a year, he and I got married.

Then he asked, "Do you want to open your own shop?" So, we went looking to find a building. Three years later, the landlord called and asked, "Are you still interested in a building?" The initial time I spoke with him, the price was too much, but this time, the price was just right. The location, space, and parking was perfect. It turned out the building was just five minutes away from home. It was perfect. I even had the support of a family member to help with securing the space.

For behold, I am for you and I will turn to you; and you shall be tilled and sown, And I will multiply men upon you, the whole house of Israel, even all of it; the cities shall be inhabited and the waste places shall be rebuilt, And I will multiply upon you man and beast, and they shall increase and be fruitful and I will cause you to be inhabited according to your former estate and I will do better for you than at your beginnings; and you shall know, understand, and realize that I am the Lord [the Sovereign Ruler, Who calls forth loyalty and obedient service.] (Ezek. 36:9– 11, amp)

6

WB
Being Driven

We as people should know that we are important. Our knowledge is needed in the world to make this world a better place. We can change the world. We are innovators and business owners. I didn't know before, but now, I can say, "Thank you, God, for making me be important enough to you to continue giving me all the pushes." I thank God for the good and for the bad pushes. It was truly a lesson learned. For the good push, I gained wisdom, and for the bad push, I gained knowledge.

My grandmother was the person who helped me to blossom to the woman I am today, and I will always remember what she taught me. I'll also always have the drive and ambition I gained by her encouragement. I always strive to do better. My grandmother Ruth Griffin-Holliday was my life. She was the lifeline for me and my sister. Gladly enough, my sister and I made a choice to make a change, or our life would have never changed.

Dwell in me, and I will dwell in you [Live in me, and I will live in you.] Just as no branch can bear fruit of itself without abiding in {begin vitally united to} the vine, neither can you bear fruit unless you abide in Me. I am the vine; you are the branches. Whoever lives in me and I in him bears much{abundant} fruit. However, apart from me [cut off from vital union with Me] you can do nothing. If you live in me [abide vitally united to me] and my words remain in you and continue to live in your hearts, ask whatever you will, and it shall be done for you. (John 15:4, 5, 7; amp) Being pushed into your destiny is love and guidance.

There will be detours, potholes, and no U-turns. Don't give up on your dreams, and always remember, with God, all things are possible if you only believe. You ask yourself, "Can any good come from being a drop out to earning a high school diploma? Could one become successful after working sixteen years on a job and led to be terminated?" I went from attending cosmetology school to working in a salon to becoming my own boss. I am the owner of Royal'ti Hair Studio. I lived in the project community housing and made my way to section 8 with government assistance and proceeded to own my own home. I lived ungodly and became a saved Christian. I was single then a girlfriend and now a wife.

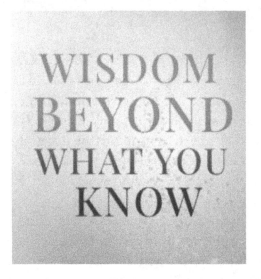

Imagine what a push can do for you with the Lord's hands on your life. I was blessed with three wonderful children, and this was an actual push. Furthermore, my children were blessed with kids of their own, and I now am a grandparent to ten grandchildren. I pray for them so that good people enter their paths to help be them travel a road map to their destiny. In each one of them, I see greatness, independence, and respect. I'm more than positive they will make great citizens of our future.

Being Pushed To Your Destiny

I'm very proud of them all. Regardless of where they are in life, I will continue to push and mold them into wonderful individuals.

Being pushed when it doesn't seem or feel right may not be the best feeling, but if you just hold on, you'll be thankful in the end.

O You sons of men, how long will you turn my honor and glory into shame? How long will you love vanity and futility and seek after lies? Selah [pause and calmly think of that]! (Ps. 4:2, amp) Allow God to be your grace, power, and sacrifice (GPS) to help you along the way, and it will get you to your destination.

We all make decisions, and it should make you stop and look at what's in front and back of you. Also, understand and know what is inside of you. You may not like it now, but it will turn out for the better. It's not bad turning a negative into a positive even if you don't see the positive in the situation. Not all mistakes will have a positive outcome, but you can always learn a lesson. We should be sensitive to God's word. I'm happy for the good, the bad, and the indifferent pushes that I received. It's all in how you receive it. If God is using you to push someone else, it's in how you give that person their push.

My road wasn't easy, and sometimes, I felt it wasn't fair. You may have lost friends, loved ones, and out of relationships, but continue to give God the praise he so very well deserves.

Blessed {happy-with life joy and satisfaction in God's favor and salvation, apart from your outward condition- and to be envied} are you when people despise{hate}you, and when they exclude and excommunicate you [as disreputable] and revile and denounce you and defame and cast out and spurn your name as evil {wicked}on account of the Son of Man. Rejoice and be glad at such a time and exult and lean for joy, for behold, your reward is rich and great and strong and intense and abundant in heaven; for even so their forefathers treated the prophets. (Luke 6:22–23)

While we look for a deep answer, God meets us where we are in life. Clearly, there is greatness in you, so let's embrace what God already knows about us all! "For I know the thoughts and plans that I have for you, says the Lord, thoughts and plans for welfare and peace and not for evil, to give you hope in your outcome" (Jer. 29:11, amp).

I'm grateful and humble enough to know that this walk thus far was not all about me. Thank you to everyone who played a part in my life and who gave me a helping hand to push me into my destiny I thank God for a recovery state of mind and a willing spirit.

I know that I had to let many opportunities go because time have been difficult however I know that I'm worthy ,don't worry because new opportunity will come to you all of them big and better than before with your personality you will meet new people you are one of the best you are full of hope you brighten up all the peoples you give people the courage to move on.

Therefore, the prisoner for the Lord, appeal to and beg you to walk (lead a life) worthy of the [divine] calling to which you have been called [with behavior that is a credit to the summons to God' service, living as becomes you] with complete lowliness of mind (humility) and meekness (unselfishness, gentleness, mildness), with patience, bearing with patience, bearing with one another and making allowances because you love one another.

Be eager and strive earnestly to guard and keep the harmony and oneness of [and produced by] the Spirit in the binding power of peace. (Eph. 4:1–3, amp)

NOTES

CPSIA information can be obtained
at www.ICGtesting.com
Printed in the USA
BVHW090444221022
649997BV00015B/1074